CALIFORNIA MISSIONS

A Guide to the State's Spanish Heritage

Jeanne Broome   CARMEL MISSION

A RENAISSANCE HOUSE PUBLICATION

Gregory Lee

2002 Printing

ISBN: 1-55838-122-8

Renaissance House Publishers
A Division of Primer Publishers
5738 North Central Avenue
Phoenix, Arizona 85012

1-800-521-9221

Cover photo of Santa Clara de Asis Mission by Glenn Matsumura, courtesy of Santa Clara University. All interior photos supplied by the missions unless otherwise noted.

10 9 8

Printed in China, Published in the United States of America

Contents

WELCOME

Wherever your travels take you along California's El Camino Real, "The Royal Highway," be sure to look for the distinctive tan road signs with the state's bear insignia. These designate the approach to one of California's State Historic Landmarks, many of which provide fascinating glimpses of 18th and 19th century life before California became a state. A visit to some of the landmarks can tell the traveler more about the history of the missions than an entire book. A trip through time along the highway allows travelers to weave the past with the present in a powerful illustration of California's history.

As you plan your visits to the missions, please note that nearly all are closed on Easter, Thanksgiving and Christmas. Most are open daily including Sundays.

This guide uses a number of Spanish terms, some of which are listed below:

Alta California: Upper California, now the state of California.

asistencia: A facility such as a chapel, rest stop or mill that serves as an annex to a nearby mission.

Baja California: Lower California, now the state of Baja in Mexico.

campanile: In the missions, an outer wall with niches for bells.

convento: The friars' quarters, usually adjacent to the mission church building.

padre: Father, in this case, a missionary of the Franciscan order of the Catholic church.

presidio: Fort, an armed outpost of Spanish soldiers who defended the lands around the missions.

pueblo: A village.

ranchero: A rancher, land owner.

rancho: Ranch; during the mission era these were vast land holdings, much larger than a typical Southern plantation of the same era, and were primarily for cattle raising.

reredos: Wall painting and altar decorations.

THE MISSION LEGACY

The 21 missions that dot the California landscape from San Diego to Sonoma are the relics of an ambitious plan in the European conquest of the New World. The program used by the Spanish to colonize California was unique among the methods tried in North America. The Spanish monarchy charged the Franciscan order of the Catholic Church, in tandem with the Spanish military, to secure the western shores of what was called New Spain, establishing missions to convert the native Indian population to Christianity. Each mission would be the beginning of a civilian town, and they would be located at regular intervals up the entire stretch of the colony. The missions' brief history is one of remarkable achievement and swift decline.

The missions were the primary centers of religious, cultural and agricultural activity. Spanish soldiers in nearby *presidios* were available for protection against other European powers, pirates and hostile natives. The padres used money donated by benefactors to begin their elaborate work, training the Indians in masonry so the missions could be raised, as well as farming and ranching, winemaking, candlemaking, and more. In return, the natives agreed to live in or around the mission, helping to maintain the fields and livestock while they learned the ways of God and the church. For both the missionaries and the Indians, adaptability to new ways was essential to survival.

Some Indians, intrigued by the padres' gifts, strange

4

language, and obvious authority, submitted to the mystical rites of baptism, Mass, and even marriage, and agreed to obey the paternal will of the padres. In return, their hard work was rewarded with regular meals and instruction. In theory, the missions and the lands they cultivated still belonged to the Christianized Indians--called "neophytes" by the padres. They were to be held in trust by the church until the Indians were capable of maintaining this new lifestyle on their own. But there were many reasons why this never happened.

While some of the native converts remained loyal to the missions, many more found the regimentation of the padres far too alien. Ultimately they became disinterested in the Christian approach to life. Another source of friction was the mistreatment of the natives by Spanish soldiers, over whom the padres had very little influence. Disease and the arrival of the white man eventually doomed the California Indian population. It is a tragic irony of the mission era that while trying to save so many pagans, it instead exposed them to deadly illnesses.

The padres' own descriptions of mission life show evidence of the harsh conditions under which the Indians often lived. Despite the hard work and occasional punishments, however, thousands of neophytes became skilled artisans and thrived in the mission system, remaining loyal to the Franciscans to the very last.

Two significant events occurred during the 1800s that affected all the missions. One was in 1812, when a series of massive earthquakes rocked California and damaged or leveled many of the first adobe sites. The second was in 1834, when Alta California was taken over by newly-independent Mexico and "secularization" was ordered. The church was now forced to give up the missions, with the holdings to be divided between the Indians and the neighboring *pueblos*. In fact, most of the missions' lands and livestock were appropriated by civilian authorities or sold for a fraction of their worth, leaving the Indians without the homes and guidance they had painfully tried to adopt. Those that hadn't perished from illness gradually disappeared. After the annexation of California by the United States, individual missions slowly were restored to the Catholic Church, but only after decades of neglect and abandonment had left most of them in ruins.

FATHER JUNIPERO SERRA

PADRE JUNIPERO SERRA

The man who is now a part of California legend was born Miguel Jose on November 24, 1713, on the island of Majorca. At 16 he entered the Franciscan Order and took the name Junipero. Even before his ordination, he became a professor of philosophy and theology, believing his life's work was to convert pagans. Another Franciscan, Francisco Palou, shared the same need for adventure, and the two joined a group of friars traveling to New Spain in 1749.

It took 99 days to reach Vera Cruz, and from here Serra made his way on foot to Mexico City. Here he spent many years in charge of the Sierra Gorda missions to the northeast. At 56, he was chosen to replace the Jesuits in Baja California and make the first land expedition with Gaspar de Portola to Alta California.

After founding the first missions, Serra made a pilgrimage back to Mexico City in 1773 to advise his superiors of what the new colony needed. His enthusiasm for the mission project and that of his successor, Padre Fermin Francisco de Lasuen, was probably the most important factor in their initial success. Serra zealously shielded the missions from the competing interests of power-hungry civilian governors and overbearing military men. His purpose was to save souls; all else was secondary.

Serra's contemporaries claim he was an eloquent preacher who wasn't above self-flagellation to emphasize his message. When he died on August 28, 1784, his legacy was secure. Padre Serra has passed several beatification hurdles, and is now one step away from canonization as a saint by the Vatican.

Gregory Lee   SAN DIEGO de ALCALA

MISSION SAN DIEGO de ALCALA

Being the first mission dedicated in Alta California, San Diego de Alcala was, not surprisingly, one of the most difficult to begin and sustain. The founding expedition led by Gaspar de Portola and Padre Serra from Baja California nearly perished on route to the site scouted by an earlier expedition. Of the three supply ships that set out to meet the overland party at what would become San Diego, one was lost with all hands, and the crews of the other two were virtually wiped out by scurvy. Nevertheless, a site was chosen and dedicated. Much work lay ahead, however, before the mission could thrive.

The mission site was moved several miles inland to its present location in 1774 when the padres decided to distance themselves from the first *presidio*, or armed outpost of the Spanish soldiers. The fathers correctly surmised that the presence of the soldiers did not help their conversion of the natives. The "neophytes," as the natives were called, were often harassed by the soldiers, and Indian women were not safe.

Outbreaks of violence in the early years were frequent and bloody. One padre was killed on November 4, 1775, when hundreds of native Indians surrounded the outpost in the dead of night, looting and setting fire to the buildings.

Earthquakes in the early 1800s twice ruined San

7

Gregory Lee   THE CAMPANILE

Diego de Alcala. This was not uncommon, however, since most of the missions suffered major earthquake damage at some time. The structure was restored in 1931. Connected directly to this simple church front is a beautiful bell wall or *campanile* containing five bells. A lovely garden lies beyond the wall.

California's first church, at Mission San Diego, is now designated a basilica because of its historic importance to the Catholic Church. Here, also, is the state's first cemetery, containing the graves of many native Indians, the first west coast victims of European diseases. One of the sad legacies of the mission program is that disease probably killed as many natives as the souls the padres claim to have saved.

The mission's original location is in San Diego's Presidio Park, near the Junipero Serra Museum. Site of the first European settlement in California, the museum overlooks the harbor area and San Diego's Old Town. Captain Portola established the Royal Presidio San Diego to protect his soldiers and the first mission. The museum houses one of the finest collections of Spanish Renaissance furniture in the United States, as well as many archaeological artifacts unearthed at both mission sites.

Location: 10818 San Diego Mission Rd., San Diego.

Founded: July 16, 1769; first in the chain.

Directions: From I-5 take I-8 E to Mission Valley. Take Mission Gorge Rd. exit N; turn L on Twain Ave. (San Diego Mission Rd.). From I-15 S, take Friars Rd. exit E; turn R on Rancho Mission.

Gregory Lee   ARCH FRAMES CALIFORNIA'S FIRST PEPPER TREE

SAN LUIS REY de FRANCIA

Nicknamed "King of the Missions," Mission San Luis Rey and its adjoining buildings occupy six acres of land, the largest in area of all the missions. It is highly visible because of its brilliant white exterior, its blue-capped bell tower and lengthy colonnade forming the front of the mission.

Founded by Padre Lasuen, the Mission San Luis Rey was named for Louis IX, a king of France and patron of the Franciscan Order. The mission grew quickly after its founding, serving the largest population of any of the missions: more than 2,700 at one time. Crops included grapes, oranges and olives, and the livestock numbered more than 50,000. Until the mid-1800s this mission's church was the largest building in California.

The missions served a wide area and sometimes the padres would build permanent chapels for conducting services. The best-known of these chapels, called *asistencias*, was at Pala, a village about 20 miles inland from the San Luis Rey Mission.

Two years after it was founded in 1816, the chapel had to be enlarged and other buildings added to house many native Indian youths. Wheat, corn, beans and garbanzos were grown in the soil at the base of Palomar Mountain. This *asistencia* has the only freestanding bell tower in the mission chain. The

9

chapel and cemetery still form the heart of this small village, which can be reached by traveling east from the mission along Highway 76 and following the signs to Pala Mission Road.

When the missions were secularized to distribute private property among the Spanish-Mexican settlers, San Luis Rey could barely care for the few hundred natives who remained. The mission decayed until 1893, when Father Joseph Jeremiah O'Keefe came to convert it into a Franciscan college. It is one of four missions still owned by the Franciscans.

The mission at San Luis Rey has an interesting self-guided museum tour through the front building, winding through an inner courtyard which allows a glimpse into the private gardens and continues through the old church and cemetery. The museum houses the largest collection of 18th-and 19th-century Spanish vestments in the United States. Other rooms display accouterments that show how the friars lived and worked. In the museum room containing religious art is a well-preserved statue of the Virgin Mary circa 1770, the year after Padre Serra began founding the mission chain of Alta California.

The church itself has many striking features. The pulpit is original, except for the overhang, and shows the Moorish influence typical in Spanish architecture of that time. This mission's dome is the only one with a wooden cupola, built from pine wood brought down from nearby Palomar Mountain, now site of the world-famous astronomical telescope and observatory. The mission also claims the only church with a double dome arrangement of wood. Six-foot-thick adobe walls are the only walls left from the original structure. The baptismal font is also original, cast from hand-hammered copper by the natives.

On the land in front of the mission are ruins of the soldiers' barracks and a sunken garden with a laundry area that served the entire population. Travelers should also visit the padres' crypt in the southwest corner of the cemetery, and the friary garden at the west end of the mission where the first pepper tree in California was planted.

Location: 4050 Mission Ave. (Hwy. 76), San Luis Rey.
Founded: June 13, 1798; 18th in the chain.
Directions: From I-5 in Oceanside, take Hwy. 76 (Mission Ave. exit) E 4 mi. to Rancho Del Oro Dr. From I-15, take Hwy. 76 (Mission Ave.) W 15 mi.

Gregory Lee   SAN JUAN CAPISTRANO

MISSION SAN JUAN CAPISTRANO

The "Jewel of the Missions," so-called because it is perhaps the best known, is the mission at San Juan Capistrano. The site is a sort of archaeological exhibit surrounded by courtyards with lovely trees, fountains and, of course, swallows. The migratory birds do, indeed, make their homes in and around this mission town, and their celebrated arrival is always feted on March 19, Saint Joseph's Day.

On this day it is customary for the mission bells to be tolled, a practice nearly as legendary as the swallows themselves. The bells are still rung by pulling ropes tied to each clapper, instead of swinging the supports above the bells, which are stationary. Two of the bells were cast in 1796, the other two in 1804. The largest is inscribed with the names of the padres who served the mission at that time. When the bell tower was destroyed, they were hung in the existing *campanile*.

The swallows who make their homes in the mission are called Las Golondrinas, but ornithologists call them cliff swallows. These are not the same as the fork-tailed or barn swallow. The majority arrive about March 19 each year after a migration of 2,000 miles from their winter homes in Central America. The birds build nests in the walls and arches of the mission using mud and saliva. Despite the presence of the swallows, it is more often pigeons that travelers feed in the courtyard!

The original Great Stone Church was designed with a floor plan shaped like a Latin cross. Construction took place from 1797 to 1806, and the padres had every intention that

11

this was to be the finest church in the mission chain. Sadly, the church and its crowning glory, a 120-foot high bell tower, were destroyed by the devastating earthquake of 1812, and no attempt was made to rebuild it. Forty bodies were pulled from the rubble, for the tragedy occurred during Mass. All that remain are the ruins, but the entire back wall of the church is still intact.

Other buildings on the property have been restored and travelers can tour the Serra Chapel, the only surviving structure in the state where Padre Serra was known to have conducted services. The highlight of this beautiful chapel is a baroque *reredos* believed to be 300 years old. It is not original to San Juan Capistrano, but was brought from Barcelona in 1906, intended for a new cathedral in Los Angeles. Instead it was put in storage and installed in 1924 in the Serra Chapel. Being a bit too wide for the chapel, it had to be trimmed. Today's visitors can view its elaborate giltwork. Travelers to the mission should give special attention to the intricate stonework on the ruined Great Stone Church. Spectacular arches, doorways, and keystones reveal the work of a great mason. In fact, the stonework has been compared favorably to that found in Roman and Greek ruins. The padres kept their promise that this Jewel of the Missions would be the showcase of their work.

The soldiers' barracks, a native American museum, and many artifacts from the rancho period are on display, making San Juan Capistrano the mission with the greatest historical variety. Outdoor furnaces for cooking and metallurgy, tanning vats for creating leather goods, and tallow ovens for making soap, candles, ointments and other necessities, are all visible by touring the grounds. Archaeological test pits have been dug at several areas around the mission to learn more about the early Californians.

By traveling northwest on I-405 to Estancia Park in Costa Mesa, you can visit the Diego Sepulveda Adobe at 1900 Adams Avenue. This home, built in the early 1800s, was first used as a shelter for Indians who tended cattle for the Capistrano Mission.

Location: Ortega Hwy. at Camino Capistrano San Juan Capistrano.

Founded: October 30, 1775, and again on November 1, 1776; seventh in the chain. The site was established by Father Larsen, but abandoned because of Indian unrest. Father Serra founded it again in 1776.

Directions: From I-5, take the Ortega Hwy. exit W to Camino Capistrano.

Gregory Lee   MISSION SAN GABRIEL GARDENS

SAN GABRIEL ARCANGEL

The site of this "Queen of the Missions" is near the aptly-named Rio de los Temblores (River of Earthquakes). Not only was Mission San Gabriel a victim of the early 19th-century tremors, it was devastated more recently by the Whittier quake of 1987. The mission, the museum and the winery were all closed for safety reasons. The church and winery did not take long to repair, but the museum reopened in 1996 after an extensive 9-year reinforcement project.

The grounds themselves are lovely, and by themselves make a visit to this mission worthwhile. The buildings reveal incredible beauty first created in the 1810s and brought back to life during recent decades. The church's fortress-like appearance, with buttresses capped by pyramid shapes, is credited to Padre Cruzado, who is said to have modeled the structure after a mosque. The brick and mortar church is the oldest of its kind south of Monterey. The structure's bell tower, lost to the earthquake of 1812, was replaced by a *campanile* containing six bells. The ruins of the bell tower are visible near the lush grapevines that cling to one side of the old church. So sturdy was the construction, however, that most of the old church survived the tremors that leveled some other missions.

Legend says that a large armed group of native Indians threatened to prevent the small founding party from dedicating this mission site. The Indians were pacified only when the padres produced a canvas painting of Our Lady of Sorrows. The 300-year-old painting is still in storage at the mission.

It had already been decided by the padres that one of the first missions should be named in honor of God's messenger angel, Gabriel. The San Gabriel Valley was later named for the area where the mission was built. In 1775, the padres decided to move to higher ground to avoid flooding from the San Gabriel River. The original site of the old mission, referred to as La Mission Vieja, can be found at the corner of North San Gabriel Boulevard and Lincoln Avenue in Montebello.

This mission was one of the more prosperous, and it thrived through the early 1800s. San Gabriel grew more wheat than any mission, and had thousands of fruit trees. At one time it boasted the largest winery in California, the grapes grown from clippings first brought by Serra himself from Europe. The floor of the building on the northeast corner, once the padres' living quarters, was inclined slightly where the grapes were trod upon by workers and the juice allowed to flow into an outside trough.

The long building once used as the missionaries' quarters, storage, and workrooms is now the museum. A highlight is the display of Gabrielino Indian paintings depicting the Fourteen Stations of the Cross. These canvases are believed to be the oldest examples of sacred art done by native California painters. Paint colors were made from crushed wildflowers and the canvas taken from sailing cloth.

A short trip from the mission is the Vigare Adobe at 616 S. Ramona Street, one of the oldest adobe structures in Los Angeles County. The Vigare Adobe was built by a soldier of the mission guard and his family lived here for several generations.

An *asistencia* of Mission San Gabriel is at the heart of downtown Los Angeles: Nuestra Senora La Reina de Los Angeles, at 535 N. Main Street. Built in 1818, this parish is near the plaza known as El Pueblo de Los Angeles. The plaza here forms the southern end of Olvera Street, a brick avenue shopping bazaar that is the site of the first adobe home in Los Angeles. Travelers can shop and dine along this charming street seven days a week.

Location: 537 W. Mission Dr., San Gabriel.
Founded: September 8, 1771; fourth in the chain.
Directions: From I-10, take the New Avenue exit N and follow the signs.

IN THE 1890s

TODAY

San Fernando Rey de Espana

This popular mission, perhaps because of its proximity to Hollywood, often is used for location shooting. It is a charming structure but, like the nearby Mission San Gabriel, has been victimized by earthquakes. The first permanent church was finished in December 1806, but reinforcement of the walls was necessary after a large quake in 1812. Deterioration in the late 1800s nearly ruined the entire site. Restoration finally was undertaken in 1923. When, in 1971, the Sylmar tremor made the church unsafe, the original structure was demolished and completely rebuilt.

Although there are many claims about who first discovered gold in California, one of the earliest finds took place near the San Fernando Mission on March 9, 1842. Francisco Lopez, the mayordomo of the mission found shiny yellow particles clinging to some roots from a bunch of onions. From then until the discovery of gold at Sutter's Mill in northern California, the Placerita Canyon area northwest of San Fernando became the focus of intense prospecting. Rumors

15

abounded that the missionaries at San Fernando had found and hoarded gold, and by the early 1900s vandals had dug holes on the deteriorated mission grounds hoping to find the "dead monks" treasure.

The most recognizable feature of the San Fernando Mission is its *convento*, or missionary quarters, which are normally connected to the church. But at this mission the *convento* is separate with a beautiful colonnade of 21 Roman arches. Completed in 1822, it served as the headquarters of Col. John C. Fremont when his army invaded California in 1847 to take control from Mexico. It also was a stop for a stage coach line. The two-story *convento* remains the largest adobe structure in California: 243 feet long, 65 feet wide, and 45 feet high.

The *convento* houses one of the oldest libraries in California, featuring books collected by the padres which were periodically moved from one seminary to another. The Archdiocese of Los Angeles ordered the collection restored, catalogued, and housed at this mission.

A relatively new feature of the mission is the Archival Center. Its purpose is to collect, restore, catalog, and display documents, manuscripts, diaries, and photographs of early California and American Catholic history and make them available to researchers by appointment.

Across the street from the mission in Brand Park are a fountain and two stone soap vats that were originally part of the courtyard. Many of the plantings in the park were brought from the Santa Barbara Mission. Also near the mission is the second-oldest house in Los Angeles, the Andres Pico Adobe. Once the home of the ranchero who owned the entire San Fernando Valley, it is now a State Historic Monument. It was built by the mission Indians, and is a finely restored example of rancho life in 19th-century California. From the mission, head west on San Fernando Blvd., turn south on Sepulveda Blvd., and proceed to 10940 Sepulveda at Brand Blvd.

Location: 15151 San Fernando Mission Blvd., Mission Hills.

Founded: September 8, 1797; 17th in the chain.

Directions: From I-5 (Golden State Fwy.), exit San Fernando Mission Blvd. and go W; from I-405 (San Diego Fwy.), exit San Fernando Mission Blvd. and go east.

G.G. Weland   VENTURA MISSION

SAN BUENAVENTURA

Originally intended as the third mission to be built, because it was halfway between San Diego and Carmel, San Buenaventura was actually the last mission to be founded during Padre Serra's lifetime. Disagreements between Serra and the civilian government often led to changing priorities, and the mission's founding was put off ultimately for 12 years. Serra wrote that the mission shared this delay in common with its namesake, Saint Bonaventure. "The longer it took, the more solemnly did we celebrate." San Buenaventura was one of six missions that Serra dedicated personally. He once held Easter Mass just north of the present mission site.

San Buenaventura Mission, meant to be the first midway stop between San Luis Obispo and San Gabriel, was located in one of the most populous regions of native California, along the shore of the Santa Barbara Channel where the Pacific Ocean separates the mainland from the Channel Islands. On Easter morning, March 31, 1782, Father Serra raised a cross at La Playa de la Canal de Santa Barbara, "the beach of the Santa Barbara Channel." Here he celebrated Mass and established Mission San Buenaventura. A cross subsequently raised on the hill nearby was destroyed by the elements in 1832, as was its successor in 1875. The present cross was erected in 1912.

The fertile land was ripe for the type of industry the padres had in mind. The soil could grow exotic fruits, including bananas and sugar cane, and in overall agricultural production, the mission ranked seventh in the chain. The mission's reputation for fruits and vegetables and its proximity to the Channel made it a popular stop for whaling vessels as they plied the coastal waterways.

17

A major reason for the success of this heavy agricultural production was irrigation. The ambitious padres built a seven-mile-long aqueduct to bring water from the Ventura River to the mission. Remnants of the aqueduct can be seen in the form of an adobe reservoir and two sections of the cobblestone-and-mortar aqueduct. The tank is located in Eastwood Park at the north end of Valdez Alley, 115 E. Main Street. The aqueduct is along Canada Larga Road. The plentiful water supply helped the mission maintain its lush orchards and gardens.

The first church building at San Buenaventura was destroyed by a fire. Only after much effort was the present church and surrounding quadrangle completed in 1809. Just three years later, the earthquakes of 1812 caused the padres to take temporary shelter a few miles inland. In 1818, the threat of pirate raids persuaded the padres to move many of the church's possessions into the foothills. After secularization the church required more restoration, yet its appearance today remains close to the original.

During two days in March 1838, two competing Mexican army factions met here. Using cannons, one lay siege to the other. The defenders inside the mission slipped away under cover of darkness, only to be captured the next day. Scars left by cannon balls in the mission walls were visible for many years.

Sometimes the zeal to restore and modernize an historic structure can ruin the appeal and original intention of its builders. San Buenaventura became a classic victim of such architectural noodling. In 1893 the resident priest insisted on improving the church with a number of decorative changes that, fortunately, have been reversed. He first ordered the windows lengthened and then filled them with very dark stained glass. He had the original Indian wall decorations painted over with Victorian-era designs. A canopied wooden pulpit was removed entirely.

The most notable external features of the mission today are the bell tower and the triangular frame on the front facade, with a window in the center. San Buenaventura is the only mission known to have had wooden bells. These curious items were carved out of blocks two-feet thick. As was done in certain parts of Mexico, the bells may have been used during Holy Week when metal bells were normally silent.

Location: 211 E. Main St., Ventura.
Founded: March 31, 1782; ninth in the chain.
Directions: From Hwy. 101 N, take California St. exit. Turn N on California St., left on Main St. From Hwy. 101 S, take Main St. exit. Right on Main St., 1.2 miles.

Santa Barbara CVB

SANTA BARBARA

Santa Barbara was the first mission founded by Padre Fermin Francisco de Lasuen, the successor to Padre Serra as presidente of the California missions. Serra had dedicated the mission site in April of 1782. But without permission from then-Governor Felipe de Neve, construction could not begin on the buildings until the *presidio* was finished, for a *presidio* always preceded the establishment of each mission. Serra died soon after permission was given to establish Mission Santa Barbara in 1784, and it was left to Padre Lasuen to continue Serra's work. Until then, the spiritual needs of the soldiers, Indians and padres had to be served by Mission San Buenaventura, founded that same year.

The reasons behind these construction delays were many, but near the end of Padre Serra's life the main reason was the jealousy of Governor Neve, who was wary of the economic power the Franciscans gained with each new mission. Unknown to Serra, Neve managed to obstruct new mission foundings as long as he stayed in office by convincing the Viceroy, his immediate boss, to withhold the needed funds. As a consequence, the three missions planned for the Channel Islands area did not materialize until after Serra was dead.

The presence of a *presidio* visible from the channel was an important step in establishing territorial rights in this part of Alta California. The Spaniards were anxious about pirates sailing up the coast and Russians sailing down. Lasuen chose a hilly site about a mile-and-a-half northeast of the *presidio*, overlooking the valley and channel named in honor of Saint Barbara. The Indians called the place Tanayan or "rocky mound." On December 4, Lasuen raised the cross and blessed the site just as Serra had done at the *presidio*. Another ceremony was held on December 16 for the benefit of the new governor, Pedro Fages. Although the governor considered December 16 the founding date, the Franciscans maintained it was December 4.

The first quadrangle of buildings and chapel at Santa Barbara was finished in 1795, after which a second quadrangle was begun adjacent to the first. A succession of ever-larger versions of the church was built from adobe, until the most elaborate one, featuring six side chapels, was finished in 1794. This structure was ruined in the earthquakes of 1812 so a new building of stone was begun. Dedicated on September 10, 1820, the new church was 161 feet long, 42 feet high, and 27 feet wide. At first the mission had one tower only, but a second was added by 1833, making it the only mission today with two towers.

The mission's facade is adapted from the design of a Roman temple the padres found in an illustrated book by Vitruvius Polion, a Roman architect. Its design is from 27 B.C. The front arcade also featured Roman-inspired arches, a remarkable feat of construction for native Chumash workers on the California frontier.

An attractive fountain with Indian-carved animal water spouts is directly in front of the mission. The large basin doubled as a *lavanderia*--a laundry for Indian women to wash clothes. Remains of two reservoirs, a millhouse, and portions of an aqueduct built by the missionaries and native Indians can be seen between the Mission Historical Park and the Santa Barbara Botanic Garden. This water system was the most elaborate of the missions, with one branch for the gardens, orchards, and laundry, and a separate branch with a filtration system for drinking.

An earthquake nearly destroyed the mission again in 1925, causing heavy damage to the front facade and towers. An expensive restoration, faithful to the original architecture, was completed in 1927. Unfortunately, a chemical reaction in the building materials weakened the restoration and 23 years later the work had to be repeated. Concrete and reinforced steel now support this mission, but the stone facade and towers appear just as they did in the mission's glory days.

Mission Santa Barbara has a royal view, sitting on its promontory above the Pacific Ocean. The neo-

Santa Barbara CVB, Tom Tuttle   MISSION SANTA BARBARA

classical interior uses imitation marble. Painted wooden statues of the saints are from the mission period in Mexico. The 18th-century canvases, including the Assumption and Coronation of the Virgin, are the largest paintings of any in the mission chain.

On display in the museum, travelers can see three stone figures of Hope, Charity, and Saint Barbara, the only surviving examples of monumental stone sculpture carved by native California Indians. The brightly painted statues originally sat atop the mission's facade; replicas are now in their place.

The archive/library dates from the mission's founding. A register containing the baptisms, marriages and deaths recorded by both Padre Serra and Padre Lasuen begins in 1782. In 1833, Padre Narciso Duran, then presidente of the missions, transferred his headquarters from Mission San Jose, bringing with him the documents relating to the entire mission chain. Santa Barbara then became the official repository for this indispensable record of California's mission era. Other rare document collections have been added to the archives, making it one of the most significant in the state. Here, too, is housed the largest known collection of sheet music from the mission era. A library wing was added in 1967 to accommodate this impressive historical collection.

Location: 2201 Laguna Street, Santa Barbara.
Founded: December 4, 1786; 10th in the chain.
Directions: From Hwy. 101 going N, take Santa Barbara St. Go S, turn L on Mission St., then L on Laguna.

21

G.G. Weland   MISSION SANTA INES

MISSION SANTA INES

The last of the missions founded in southern California, Santa Ines is one of three named for a woman. Saint Agnes was a 13-year-old martyr who died in Rome in 304 A.D. Despite the Santa Ynez Valley's pretty setting, there were few travelers to the mission because the site was not close to El Camino Real.

The original church was erected between 1805-1812, but earthquakes promptly ruined it and the adjoining buildings. The new church was finally dedicated in 1817. California's first seminary was later founded here. The Santa Ines mission buildings are in an L-shape, forming one-third of the original quadrangle which is now gone. The church building is simple in design. Indian murals, some of which can still be seen, decorate the church interior. Other Indian paintings can be seen in the museum along with many artifacts, paintings and sculptures.

In 1824, when Spain cut off mission funding following Mexican independence, the missions had to support their garrisoned soldiers. Native labor became more important to survival, yet the soldiers' abuses of the natives increased. Shortly, two revolts erupted in Santa Ines and neighboring La Purisima Concepcion, with much damage to both sides. Although the mission experienced the usual decay after secularization, Santa Ines was never completely abandoned.

Location: 1760 Mission Drive, Solvang.
Founded: September 17, 1804; 19th in the chain.
Directions: From Hwy. 101 in Buellton, exit Hwy. 246 and go E 3 mi. to Solvang. From Hwy. 154, head W on Hwy. 246 to Solvang.

LA PURISIMA

La Purisima is another of the Franciscan missions located off the beaten path of El Camino Real. When it was first founded by Padre Lasuen, some 100 adobe buildings were built by the missionaries and the Chumash Indians. But the earthquakes of 1812, followed by winter rains did so much damage to the original mission that its location was changed to the present site, four miles northeast of Lompoc in La Canada de los Berros, "Canyon of the Watercress".

The La Purisima area was very good for ranching. Thousands of livestock ranged here during the mission's heyday. Shops for weaving, pottery and leatherwork were integrated with the religious activities of the mission. The secularization of 1834 put the mission into private hands and eventually the entire facility collapsed. In 1933 the property was donated to the public by the Union Oil Company. The area surrounding the mission is now a 966-acre state historic park with ten fully restored buildings--the most complete restoration of the 21 missions. Travelers can see 37 rooms furnished in period style, as well as many unrestored ruins. The site retains much of its original appearance.

Mission volunteers, the Prelado de los Tesoros or "Keeper of the Treasures," assume character roles and costumes from 1820, providing information and tours to travelers in period style.

Location: 2295 Purisima Road, Lompoc. Original site ruins are at 508 South "F" St. & East Locust, Lompoc.
Founded: December 8, 1787; 11th in the chain.
Directions: From Hwy. 101 in Buellton, exit Hwy. 246 and go W 15 mi. to Purisima Road. From Hwy. 1 in Lompoc, go E on Hwy. 246 to Mission Gate Rd.

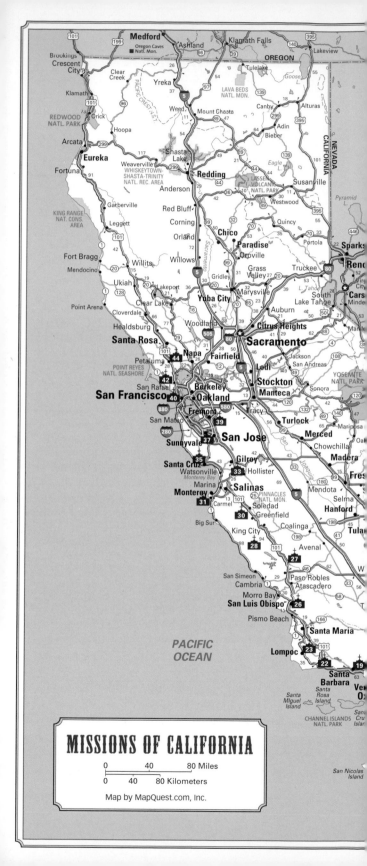

MISSIONS OF CALIFORNIA

```
0        40        80 Miles
0     40     80 Kilometers
```

Map by MapQuest.com, Inc.

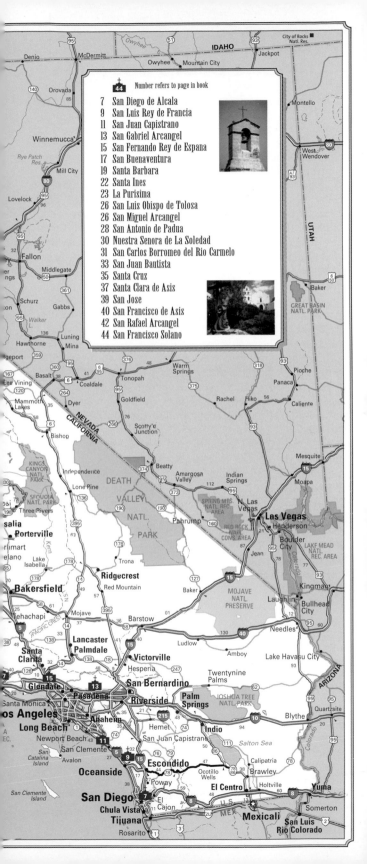

SAN LUIS OBISPO de TOLOSA

So plentiful were the bears in the valley where this mission is located that it was dubbed the "valley of the bears" by Gaspar de Portola when his expedition first arrived. Local Indians were greatly impressed with the Spaniards' ability to shoot the animals with their guns, and so provide a lot of good meat for all.

Padre Serra christened this mission in the name of Saint Louis, Bishop of Toulouse (b. 1274). The early years were not easy. After the Indians set fire to the roof for the third time, the padres developed a red, fire-resistant, clay tile which proved a good deterrent to the arsonists. Henceforth all missions after 1784 used the new formula for roofing material. Red clay tile roofs are now common in California.

San Luis Obispo's church has a belfry and vestibule combination that is unique among the missions. Three bells hang from openings directly above the church entrance. The *convento* collonade in the front has square openings and round pillars, a style not used in any other mission. For a time this unusual architecture was obscured by a New England-style steeple and white-painted siding that was added in 1880. This comical grafting job was finally dismantled and the original appearance restored in 1934.

To benefit the more distant natives, an outpost was created, the *asistencia* of Santa Margarita. Ruins of the chapel and a storehouse are visible by taking Hwy. 1 north from San Luis Obispo, then Hwy. 58 east to Santa Margarita.

Location: 782 Monterey, San Luis Obispo.
Founded: September 1, 1772; fifth in the chain.
Directions: From Hwy. 101 take the Broad St. exit and follow the signs; located between Chorro and Broad.

SAN MIGUEL ARCANGEL

The padres chose the sites of their missions so there would be only a day's journey between them. Thus San Miguel was midway between the missions at San Luis Obispo and San Antonio de Padua in Jolon. San Miguel boasts one of the better-preserved interiors, particularly the church itself. Built between 1816-18 it measures 144 feet long by 40 feet high. Its roof shows exposed woodwork of high quality.

Adorning the walls are the creations of Monterey artist Esteban Munras, who completed his work in 1821 with the help of the natives. This artwork, preserved in

MISSION SAN LUIS OBISPO

its original form, is unique among the missions. Scenes show false balconies and pillars, leaves and tassels, and imitation marble. An "all-seeing eye of God" looms above the altar, its rays of light shining in all directions. Graves of the early padres dot the sanctuary floor. The original chapel at San Miguel, erected in 1798, served until 1806 when a fire destroyed two rows of adjacent buildings and much of the mission's harvest. Other missions helped with San Miguel's immediate restoration.

After secularization the mission was used as a private residence. Later, rooms were rented and the buildings used variously as a saloon, dance hall, and general store. An old beehive oven highlights the kitchen. On display in the arcade is a cannon cast in Spain in 1697.

Location: 801 Mission St., San Miguel.
Founded: July 25, 1797; 16th in the chain.
Directions: From Hwy. 101, exit at San Miguel and follow the signs to Mission St. on the south end of town.

SAN ANTONIO de PADUA

SAN ANTONIO de PADUA

This pretty little mission is nestled in the foothills of the Santa Lucia mountains, which the padres called the "valley of the oaks." Padre Serra himself hung a bell from an oak tree in 1771 and rang it vigorously hoping, he said, to attract "All the Gentiles" within earshot. This was to be the first mission between Carmel and San Diego, and perhaps Serra considered the founding of San Antonio a further reassurance that the mission chain was becoming a reality.

When Serra returned in 1772 to check on the progress of the settlers, he found they had nearly starved. Fortunately, the neighboring Salinan Indians had, in a gesture reminiscent of the Pilgrims' first Thanksgiving, provided enough of their own forage to keep their new neighbors alive.

Deciding a site further north in Los Robles Valley would offer a better water supply, the padres erected a small adobe church, with wooden houses for the soldiers. A larger church wasn't begun until 1810. It took several years for its population to exceed 1,000 natives. Thanks to the engineering prowess of Padre Sitjar, the nearby San Antonio River was dammed, providing an excellent water system that powered the grist mill. The mission also became known for its horse breeding stock.

Much of the mission began to crumble after

MISSION SAN ANTONIO IN WINTER

secularization. In the early 1900s some partial restoration took place, but an earthquake ruined what progress had been made. The present structure with its quadrangle was nicely restored in the late 1940s, along with a gristmill, water wheel, and tannery. An excavation site marks the spot of the old adobe soldiers' barracks.

San Antonio de Padua is charming, with its mission bells hanging in the front facade above the arches of the church. Here was where the first Christian marriage ceremony in California was performed. Here, too, was the first aqueduct in the state and the first water-powered gristmill. According to Fr. Serra, San Antonio was the first mission to have a tile roof. Its setting and proximity to El Camino Real give travelers a vivid impression of life in simpler times. California poppies and lupines bloom in the surrounding fields.

For a spectacular scenic drive, head west from Jolon on Naciamento-Fergussen Road which winds 28 miles through the mountains, emerging at Hwy. 1 on the coast. The southern route goes to San Simeon and Hearst Castle; the northern option to Big Sur and Carmel winds along some of the most gorgeous coastline in America.

Location: Hunter Liggett Military Reservation, Jolon.
Founded: July 14, 1771; third in the chain.
Directions: From Hwy. 101 N near Bradley, take Jolon Rd. W 26 mi. to Jolon. Turn L onto army base. Go 6 mi. From Hwy. 101 S just N of King City, take Jolon Rd. W 18 mi. to Jolon. From Jolon, follow the signs.

Gregory Lee   MISSION SOLEDAD

Nuestra Senora de la Soledad

The name of this mission tells its story; Padre Lasuen dedicated the site to "the solitude of Most Holy Mary, Our Lady." It was, indeed, a desolate place. The only mission in the Salinas Valley, it lies midway between the mission at Carmel to the northwest, and San Antonio de Padua to the south.

The toughest opposition to the success of Mission Soledad came from the weather. Summers in the Salinas Valley were hot and winter nights freezing. The padres complained of dampness and rheumatism. At least twice the chapel had to be rebuilt when the Salinas and Arroyo Seco Rivers flooded. Nevertheless, the padres prevailed, eventually recording more than 2,000 baptisms and 700 marriages at the mission.

Mission Soledad is the final resting place of California's first Spanish governor, Jose Joaquin Arrillaga. His grave beneath the chapel floor was only recently located and marked. The Lonely Lady of the missions felt the worst of the secularization period, beginning in 1835 with the death of Padre Vicente Sarria. No priest replaced him, and when the lands around Soledad were sold, the livestock and other valuables gradually disappeared, leaving the mission buildings to crumble in the sun for the next 100 years.

In 1954, the Native Daughters of the Golden West began dusting off what was left of Mission Soledad. A small wing of seven rooms and a single chapel are the only remnants of Soledad's history. The traditional quadrangle is gone but can still be traced in lines of sunbaked adobe ruins.

Location: 36641 Fort Romie Rd., Soledad.
Founded: October 9, 1791; 13th in the chain.
Directions: From Hwy. 101, take Arroyo Seco exit S of Soledad. Turn R on Fort Romie Rd.

Jeanne Broome   CARMEL MISSION

San Carlos Borromeo
del rio Carmelo

Carmel was the second mission founded by Padre
Serra in California. Upon his arrival at Monterey Bay
aboard the *San Antonio*, Serra blessed the ground and
hung a bell from an old oak tree. This site is now the
home of the Royal Presidio Chapel, the only remaining
structure from the original presidio (550 Church Street
near Figueroa, Monterey).

Mission Carmel was moved south of Monterey Bay
in 1771 to a location with better soil. Temporary
shelters of wood were erected, and around the complex
was built a palisade, a fence of poles sharpened at the
top.

Serra made Carmel his headquarters for the rest of
his California missionary work. When Padre Lasuen
succeeded Serra as presidente of the Alta and Baja
California missions, he supervised the building of the
present stone church in place of the adobe one in 1793.
Sandstone quarried from the neighboring Santa Lucia
Mountains was used for this beautiful structure, with its
tower of Moorish design. The interior walls curve
inward as they rise toward the ceiling, forming an arch,
and are covered with a lime plaster made from burnt
seashells.

It took four years to erect the structure, which

Jeanne Broome   MISSION GROUNDS

finally was dedicated in 1797. A side chapel was added
in 1821 to serve as a mortuary for the native
population. The cemetery is said to contain the remains
of more than 3,000 California Indians.

More than 4,000 natives were baptized from the
time the mission was founded through 1836. But by
1823 the population had started to dwindle, and only a
few hundred were left when the mission was secularized in
1834.

The church and its quadrangle fell into decay until
1884, when Father Casanova took charge of restoration. A
different roof was put on the mission, which changed
the original architectural design but saved the church
from further deterioration. The first room of the old
quadrangle was restored in the early 1920s and a
memorial was created to honor the padres buried at
Carmel. Restoration has continued since the 1930s, and
in 1960 Pope John XXIII designated Carmel Mission a
minor basilica.

Padre Serra, who died in 1784, was buried next to
his associate, Padre Crespi, within the walls of the
church. Serra seemingly reserved the best spot as his
final resting place, for Carmel is one of the most scenic
places along the California coast. The mission complements
its surroundings nicely, and is a favorite of many
travelers.

Location: 3080 Rio Rd., Carmel.
Founded: June 3, 1770; second in the chain.
Directions: From Hwy. 1 S of Monterey, take the Rio
Rd. exit W 1/2 mi. to Lasuen Dr.

SAN JUAN BAUTISTA

The base of the hill below the cemetery wall at San Juan Bautista is a point of interest for travelers to California's earthquake country. The mission sits on the San Andreas fault! This singular location in the middle of the San Juan Valley meant a lot of shaky days for the missionaries. During October 1798 the padres slept out-of-doors while the ground shook repeatedly-- as often as six times a day. Huge cracks appeared, both on the grounds and in the buildings of the mission.

The existing church was dedicated in 1812, and the interior completed in 1816, much of it painted by an American sailor who jumped ship in Monterey. With three aisles or naves, San Juan Bautista is now the largest of the mission churches. Today, the mission has only half of its original buildings left. The traditional quadrangle of rooms is gone except for two sides, the *convento* wing, and the church itself.

The facade of the present mission is rather plain, a simple archway entrance with a square window above. Inside, the church has been restored to its original form, but at one time the aisles on either side of the center nave were walled off to create separate rooms. The great San Francisco quake of 1906 levelled the outer walls, and they remained unrepaired until the mid-1970s. At that time the walls were restored, the archways opened up, and the three-nave interior revealed again to create the widest church in the mission chain. The current bell wall by the entrance, while an honest imitation of architectural motifs during

33

the mission era, was never a part of the original mission.

Six statues of saints dominate the back wall of the altar, one being a life-size image of John the Baptist. On the red tile floor along the center aisle can be seen the tracks of bear and coyote, apparently made while the tiles were fresh and still drying in the sun.

San Juan Bautista has never been without a resident padre, one of the few missions that can make that claim. Padre Estevan Tapis, who founded Mission Santa Ines while serving as presidente of the missions, retired to San Juan and dedicated himself to music. The mission is now nicknamed the "Mission of Music," because its choir was among the best along El Camino Real. One of Padre Tapis' handwritten choir books, on display in the museum, shows his fascinating method of notating music: the notes are in four colors, one for each singing part.

The unusual barrel organ in the mission played tunes from wooden drums inserted with pins, much like paper rolls are used in a player piano. This delightful instrument is credited with having saved the mission from an Indian attack. Some hostile Tulare Indians were bearing down on the mission, the story goes, when one padre struck up a tune and the mission Indians began to sing. Their singing charmed the Tulares, and there was no further violence that day.

The Spanish plaza in front of the mission is the only original one remaining in California. In fact, the town square is a State Historic Park. Travelers can take a walking tour of the surrounding 12-block area, visiting some three dozen historic buildings.

This historic plaza in front of the mission helps the traveler visualize life during California's mission era. Just north of the cemetery is an original section of El Camino Real, the first road in the state. This "royal road" or "King's Highway" was the link from mission to mission and is still marked in many places along U.S. 101.

Location: 2nd and Mariposa Sts., San Juan Bautista.
Founded: June 24, 1797; 15th in the chain.
Directions: From Hwy. 101, take Hwy. 156 or San Juan Hwy. E to the town square of San Juan Bautista.

MISSION SANTA CRUZ

MISSION SANTA CRUZ

"I found the site to be most excellent as had been reported to me. I found, besides, a stream of water very near, copious and important. On August 28th, the day of St. Augustine, I said Mass and raised the cross on the spot where the mission is to be."

So wrote Father Lasuen about the humble beginnings of Mission Santa Cruz, or "Mission of the Holy Cross." The stream the padre mentioned is the San Lorenzo River, and the church sits on the gentle slopes where glorious redwoods meet the nearby Pacific Ocean.

Despite its lush surroundings, the mission had few natives to Christianize, and never had more than 400 to 500 Indians living in its parish. Because of Santa Cruz's distance from El Camino Real, Mission Santa Clara to the northeast received much more attention.

The proximity of a pueblo called Branciforte added to Santa Cruz's problems by breeding disputes between the Indians and the local Spanish settlers. A mission was supposed to have at least a league of land to itself. Experience had taught the padres that this separation was important to maintain autonomy and help settlers resist the temptation to abuse the Indians. But the governor had ignored this law by permitting a settlement on Mission Santa Cruz's lands.

With the pueblos at Los Angeles and San Jose doing poorly, then-governor Diego Borica insisted that settlers from Guadalajara help colonize the north. These people were little better than convicts, much like those who were sent to Australia from England, and they were not lovers of agricultural pursuits.

One day in 1818 there were reports that Bouchard, the pirate, was off the coast. When the padres retreated to Santa Clara for safety, the mission's valuables were plundered--not by the pirate, but by the residents of the pueblo. The friction between the church and the civilian population continued, and the mission never recovered. Santa Cruz was one of the first to be hit by secularization, and the lands went to influential families instead of the neophyte Indians.

The church, dedicated in May 1794, measured 112 feet by 30 feet, with a vaulted roof 30 feet high. But this structure did not survive the many ravages of earthquakes and Pacific storms. The bell tower fell in 1840 when a particularly fierce quake produced massive flooding. By 1857 the entire mission was in shambles, its building materials confiscated for other uses.

The 1931 replica that was built to honor the Santa Cruz mission is only half the size of the original. Its facade above the arched doorway is triangular, with a small window in the middle.

The Neary-Hopcroft Adobe, built in the early 1790s, probably housed the mission guard. It stands nearby at 130 School Street. Ironically, although the mission received no respect while it stood, its name, Santa Cruz, was given to the town that surrounds it today.

Mission Santa Cruz became, indirectly, the cause of the first autopsy in California medical history. The mission Indians were severely restricted in order to keep them away from the unsavory citizens of Branciforte. Some believed they were the victims of excessive cruelty, and one day a padre was found dead in his bed. Death was assumed to be from natural causes, but two years later a thorough investigation and autopsy were conducted, and seven Indians were eventually charged with murder. Their sentence: severe flogging.

Location: 126 High St., Santa Cruz.
Founded: September 25, 1791; 12th in the chain.
Directions: From Hwy. 1, follow Half Moon signs to Mission St. Turn L. After 2 blocks turn L again at Emmett St.

Glenn Matsumura   SANTA CLARA de ASIS

MISSION SANTA CLARA de ASIS

The first mission to honor a woman, St. Clare of Assisi, Mission Santa Clara might be called the most persistent of the 21 missions. The present location is the fifth site in its history, and the church is in its sixth version. The first mission, marked by a plaque at Kifer Rd. and De la Cruz Blvd., was built too close to the banks of the Guadalupe River and flood threats changed the minds of the padres. They picked a temporary location farther south, today's Martin Ave. and De la Cruz Blvd. Finally they agreed upon a third site, now 490 Lincoln St., that was blessed by Padre Serra himself. This site was good for 34 years.

An adobe church, 100 feet long with four-foot-thick walls was completed in May 1784. But a severe earthquake in 1818 forced construction of a temporary adobe church nearby until the fifth and present mission site was picked and construction began in 1822. Various "remodelings" occurred, including the addition of twin bell towers, until a fire in 1926 razed the entire structure.

The building that stands on the Santa Clara campus today was dedicated in 1928, and is an enlarged replica of the 1822 mission. Decorations inside the church are close duplications of the original *reredos* and the painted ceiling. But "duplication" does not, of course, mean "original." This mission is a prime example of how contemporary artists and historians collaborate in an attempt to re-create the mission era in its heydey.

Gregory Lee   MISSION SAN JOSE >>>

The roof contains more than 12,000 tiles salvaged from the earlier buildings, some as old as 1790. The wooden cross in front of the church entrance is from the original 1777 mission. From the 1822 mission, all that remain are the Adobe Lodge and Wall.

The Alameda, where the mission is located, means literally "a tree-lined avenue". The padre responsible for this inspired path was Magin Catala, the "Holy Man of Santa Clara." He had the four-mile road between Santa Clara and San Jose planted with shady black willows, hoping to encourage travelers to make the journey to the mission.

In 1851, Mission Santa Clara became the location of the first college in California. Although the Jesuits had been banned originally from the Alta California mission project by the Spanish monarchy, the new college was Jesuit. Its growth helped spare the mission from the decay that befell others during the late 1800s. The school is now Santa Clara University and the mission doubles as the chapel.

Santa Clara's records tell one of the saddest parts of the Spanish colonization. The immigrants to the Santa Clara Valley brought more than their share of smallpox and measles with them, and the native population had little resistance to these diseases. Mission Santa Clara led the other missions in burials as well as baptisms. The remains of these neophytes are in the walled rose garden right next to the mission.

Mission artifacts can be seen in the De Saisset Museum, diagonally opposite the mission church plaza. Here bullfights were actually held during the 1840s.

Location: 500 El Camino Real, Santa Clara.
Founded: January 12, 1777; eighth in the chain.
Directions: Located on the Santa Clara University campus; use I-280 or I-880, Hwy. 17 or Hwy. 101. Follow the signs to The Alameda and the campus.

MISSION SAN JOSE

In 1797, Padre Lasuen set out from Santa Cla[...] an armed guard and chose an area on the east s[...] San Francisco Bay to found a new mission. [...] Franciscans had spent so much time on the wes[...] side of the Bay that it was nearly 20 years before th[...] paid much attention to the eastern portion. Within [...] month, Padre Lasuen would also found Mission San [...] Juan Bautista to the south.

Located just 15 miles off El Camino Real, the Mission of Saint Joseph promised to be an exciting outpost for the padre who could tame its surroundings. In its day it was one of the most successful missions in the chain. But now, although it is no longer in the wilderness and surrounded by one of California's larger cities, it is very often overlooked by travelers.

But there was a time when Mission San Jose was prosperous and crowded. With more than 6,000 converts, it ranked third among the missions, after Santa Clara and San Gabriel. It also had some of the largest livestock herds and an excellent agricultural output.

This mission, perhaps more than any other, served as a base for military operations against inland tribes who were particularly hostile to the colonial intrusion. This was the only place in California where the Spaniards ventured into the interior without first securing the cooperation of the natives. Frequent raids and skirmishes resulted.

An industrious French priest tried to modernize the church in 1859 by removing some vital reinforcement that left it vulnerable to a large quake in 1868. This was the coup de grace. So much damage was done that only the padres' living quarters were left standing.

In 1985 a reconstruction of the mission church was finally completed, thanks to the efforts of archaeologists and fund raisers. Architects used real adobe bricks of uneven sizes, and period tools were employed to give the authentic appearance of a typical early 1800s building. Roof lines, tiled floors, and wall details are rough and uneven--on purpose. Some of the interior *reredos* are resplendent in 23-karat gold leaf. This painstaking attention to detail makes San Jose a must-see on any mission traveler's list.

Location: 43300 Mission Blvd., Fremont.
Founded: June 11, 1797; 14th in the chain.
Directions: From I-880 or Hwy. 680 in Fremont, use the Mission Blvd. exit (Hwy. 238) and follow the signs to the intersection of Mission and Washington Blvds.

San Francisco CVB, Christopher Ebert   MISSION DOLORES

SAN FRANCISCO de ASIS

It was not until Gaspar de Portola's second expedition in 1769 that San Francisco Bay was discovered. The Bay's importance as a naval base was immediately apparent to the Spaniards, and they decided to establish a *presidio*, pueblo, and mission as soon as possible. Explorer Juan Bautista de Anza went ahead to scout a good location for the new mission.

Guiding some 200 settlers, soldiers, and 1,000 head of livestock he marched from northwestern Mexico to Monterey in 1775-76. So successful was this expedition that babies were actually born on the journey. The spot he located he called Arroyo de los Dolores.

Padre Francisco Palou, an assistant of Padre Serra, celebrated Mass under a small shelter at the site on June 29, 1776, five days before the signing of the Declaration of Independence. But the original site proved too swampy, and in 1782 a permanent church was begun, which took nine years to build.

Mission Dolores, as it is popularly known, is the oldest intact building in San Francisco. So well did the Indian neophytes build the adobe church that it withstood the famous 1906 earthquake. In the late 1860s, a larger church was built next to the old mission church and was dedicated in 1876. It was designated as a *basilica* by Pope Pius XII in 1952. This honor is signified by the red and gold umbrella and carved coat

40

of arms to the left and right of the altar in the *b*

Inside the *basilica*, the window above the cho
shows St. Francis of Assisi. The lower windows pr
the 21 California missions. On the ceiling of the
mission are replicas of original Indian designs pain
with vegetable dyes. The museum holds artifacts th
were gifts from Padre Serra, and the baptismal registe
dates from 1776.

Within the mission quadrangle is the Lourdes
shrine, built to honor the 5,000 Indians who died from
smallpox. The cemetery once covered a larger area
than it does now. Some of the people buried in the
Mission Dolores cemetery include Luis Antonio
Arguello, the first governor of Alta California under
Mexican rule, and Francisco de Haro, the first *alcalde*
(mayor) of San Francisco. The remaining grave
markers date from the Gold Rush days, when San
Francisco was the boom town port of entry for fortune
hunters.

The San Francisco mission was not the most
successful outpost of native conversion. The damp
weather did not appeal to the Indians, and measles
epidemics buried more than 5,000 natives. So common
was illness among the Indians that the padres established
a hospital on a site north of the mission. Originally this
facility served as a sort of annex to the San Francisco
center. Later, when the population of Indians and
settlers increased, Mission San Rafael Arcangel (see p.
42), was established here.

Mission Dolores created a rancho down the
peninsula at a site now marked by the Sanchez Adobe,
a home built by a one-time mayor of San Francisco.
The five-acre site was a Costanoan Indian village
before it became an agricultural outpost of the mission
in 1786. The adobe was built in the 1840s and is nicely
restored, with archaeological displays and furnishings
from the period. The Sanchez Adobe is at 1000 Linda
Mar Blvd. at Adobe Dr. in Linda Mar, just off Hwy. 1.

Location: 3321 16th Street, San Francisco.
Founded: October 9, 1776; sixth in the chain.
Directions: From Hwy. 101 S/Bay Bridge, take Mission-Van Ness St. exit. Turn L on Mission St., then R on 16th St. two blocks to Dolores. From Hwy. 101 N, take Lombard St. Turn R on Steiner, which merges with Sanchez. Turn L on 16th St. two blocks to Dolores.
This is the northern terminus of El Camino Real, the King's Highway, which linked the 10 missions established by Padre Serra.

Marin Co. Chamber of Commerce   MISSION SAN RAFAEL

SAN RAFAEL ARCANGEL

For its first few years, San Rafael was an *asistencia* of
Mission Dolores, and its Indians counted among the
San Francisco Mission population. The site was a
convalescent hospital for neophytes weakened by the
damp climate of the bayside mission. It was decided
that a place of healing was urgently needed if the
converts were to be kept, and the northern peninsula of
the bay was noticeably warmer. The padres dubbed the
site after the arcangel whose name means "healing
power of God" and packed off the ailing to San Rafael.

A sanitarium, chapel, storeroom and monastery
made up the small, plain facility, which finally
graduated to full mission status in October 1822. It was
during this year that California came under Mexican
rule and the fate of the missions became doubtful.

For a time, one padre predicted that both Mission
Dolores and San Rafael would eventually close, with
only the new Sonoma mission (p.44) to the north
serving the Bay area, but this never happened. The
presence of the missions was important in reinforcing
Mexico's hold on this part of Alta California, where
Russian fur trappers were still encroaching and a
Russian settlement was founded at Bodega Bay.

Mission San Rafael and Mission Sonoma appear as
afterthoughts compared to the first 19 missions. San

Marin Co. Chamber of Commerce · SAN RAFAEL ARCANGEL

Rafael had no elaborate architectural plans such as the traditional quadrangle and there was no time for artistic embellishment. This mission existed only 10 years before it became the first to be secularized and its lands confiscated in 1833. The mission was abandoned, and what was left was torn down by 1870. Not one remnant of San Rafael remained.

It wasn't until 1909 that a history group, the Native Sons of the Golden West, took the first steps toward restoration by marking the old site with a mission bell sign. A replica was finally built in 1949, imitating known details of the original mission such as small star-shaped windows and a bell hung from cross beams rather than within a tower of its own. But the mission is by no means a completely faithful restoration of the original building.

At its height, San Rafael had nearly 1,000 Miwok Indians, who were compelled to work on the lands after they were taken over by the new territorial commander, General Mariano Vallejo. Secularization was supposed to return many of the mission's assets to the natives, but General Vallejo appropriated them instead for safekeeping or for national defense.

Location: 1104 Fifth Avenue, San Rafael.
Founded: December 14, 1817; 20th in the chain.
Directions: From Hwy. 101 in San Rafael, take the 5th Ave. exit and head W to A Street.

Sonoma Valley Visitors Bureau   SONOMA MISSION

SAN FRANCISCO SOLANO

The last and northernmost of the California missions was founded in 1823 when a Franciscan named Jose Altimira decided to start one without the approval of the mission presidente. This mission was the only one founded under California's Mexican period and it shares its brief history with the transition of California from "New Spain" to a part of independent Mexico.

Altimira believed a location with a warmer climate, north of the Bay Area, might help to keep his Indian neophytes healthy. He also expected that the San Rafael and Dolores missions would be closed in favor of his new one. But in this he was mistaken, and without the force of a *presidio* full of soldiers, his mission failed.

Amazingly, the current presidente did agree to let the Solano Mission stay, and soon a wooden church, granary and missionary quarters were built. Even the Russians, whose expansionist ideas threatened the mission area, donated useful items such as copper basins, linens and bells!

The mission was named after the Peruvian Indian apostle Saint Francis Solano. Surrounding fields ultimately made excellent orchards for fruit trees and grapevines.

Despite claims to have converted more than 1,300 natives, Padre Altimira was not popular with the

Indians, for he believed that moral instruction was more effective when accompanied by flogging and imprisonment. The Indians, taking advantage of the fact that there was no armed guard, ransacked the mission and forced Padre Altimira to seek safety in San Rafael. Altimira was replaced by Fr. Fortuny who had more benevolent ways and completed the 27-room mission quadrangle by 1833. The new quarters were all adobe, on 10,000 acres, and housed up to 1000 neophytes. Ultimately the mission was swallowed by secularization. After its 11 short years, it become an ordinary parish church.

The church that stands today is from the 1840s and is attached to the original mission quadrangle. General Mariano Vallejo, just 25 years old, used the quarters for his military command, and at the same time became owner of a 66,000-acre rancho. General Vallejo was charged with keeping order in this part of the Mexican territory, and was responsible for expanding colonization. He founded pueblos at Sonoma, Petaluma and Santa Rosa, at the same time confiscating the Sonoma Mission vineyards. Ultimately the vineyards would make the most lasting impression on travelers to this part of California.

Wine making was just as important to the padres as candle making or tanning. Wine was crucial to the sacrament symbolizing the blood of Christ celebrated during Catholic Mass. But wine was also the beverage of choice for the settlers of the 18th century. Mission San Gabriel was the most noteworthy of the southern wineries, and the padres had eight stills there for the making of brandy, the liquor made from grape wine.

In the early part of this century, Italian immigrant Samuele Sebastiani bought the land and began producing excellent wines. The Sonoma Valley and the neighboring Napa Valley to the east are renown, for the climate is perfect for growing a variety of grapes. The Sebastiani Vineyard is a favorite with wine country travelers, for they can see an Indian artifact museum as part of the winery tour.

Mission Solano is now part of a larger State Historic Park, which includes the Sonoma Barracks, the General Vallejo Home, the Jack London State Historic Park and Petaluma Adobe.

Location: 20 E. Spain St., Sonoma.
Founded: 1823; 21st and last in the chain.
Directions: From Hwy. 101, take Hwy. 116 E to the Sonoma Valley. In Sonoma, the mission is on the corner of 1st Street East and E. Spain St.

Santa Barbara CVB   A MISSION QUEEN ON THE KING'S HIGHWAY

EL CAMINO REAL

El Camino Real or "The Royal Road" is also nicknamed "The King's Highway." This famous California roadway runs the length of the state, from San Diego to Sonoma, linking the "jewels" of the mission chain. Later, the name was often translated as the "public highway"--purposely ignoring the term "royal" as California became a republic and then a state.

It was once just a foot trail. But as settlements and missions were established and the population grew, the trail became the main inland route for travelers. It was a stage line and eventually a highway, U.S. 101. With only a few detours, the present U.S. 101 is identical to the route the padres used. Its official historic marking is a mission bell the color of tarnished copper, arched over a sign post with the words, "El Camino Real."

Not located on the Royal Road are two missions attempted in southeastern California. These projects were unsuccessful forays into the uninviting desert, where both converts and natural resources were scarce and inhospitable. One of them, La Purisima Conception, (same name as the San Luis Obispo County mission), was begun in 1780 by Padre Francisco Garces near what is now the California-Arizona-Mexico border in Imperial County. The mission didn't last 12 months.

An even less successful site was Mission San Pedro Y San Pablo de Bicuner, also in Imperial County. A pueblo and mission were founded here on January 7, 1781. But when, on July 17, Quechan Indians attacked this would-be settlement and La Purisima Conception, the Spaniards abandoned the site.

INTERIOR, CARMEL MISSION

NAMES & NUMBERS

(p. 7) Mission San Diego de Alcalá
10818 San Diego Mission Road
Mission Valley, CA 92108
619-281-8449

(p. 8) The Junipero Serra Museum
2727 Presidio Drive
San Diego, CA 92103
619-297-3258   closed Mondays

(p. 9) Mission San Luis Rey de Francia
4050 Mission Avenue
San Luis Rey, CA 92068
760-757-3651

(p. 9) Asistencia de San Antonio de Pala
Pala Mission Road
Pala, CA 92059
760-742-1600

(p. 11) Mission San Juan Capistrano
PO Box 697
Ortega Hwy & Camino Capistrano
San Juan Capistrano, CA 92693
949-248-2048

(p. 12) Diego Sepulveda Adobe
1900 Adams Avenue
Costa Mesa, CA 92626
714-631-5918

(p. 13) Mission San Gabriel Arcángel
537 West Mission Drive
San Gabriel, CA 91776
626-457-3048

(p. 14) Vigare Adobe
616 South Ramona Street
San Gabriel, CA 91776

(p. 15) San Fernando Rey de España
15151 San Fernando Mission Blvd.
Mission Hills, CA 91345
818-361-0186

(p. 16) Andres Pico Adobe
10940 Sepulveda Blvd
Mission Hills, CA 91345
818-365-7810

(p. 17) Mission San Buenaventura
225 East Main Street
Ventura, CA 93001
805-648-4496

(p. 19) Old Mission Santa Bárbara
2201 Laguna Street
Santa Barbara, CA 93105
805-682-4713

(p. 22) Old Mission Santa Inés
Highway 246
Solvang, CA 93463
805-688-4815

(p. 23) La Purísima Mission SHP
2295 Purísima Road
Lompoc, CA 93436
805-733-3713

Gregory Lee   STATUE OF PADRE SERRA

NAME & NUMBERS

(p. 26) San Luis Obispo de Tolosa
782 Monterey
San Luis Obispo, CA 93401
805-543-6850

(p. 26) Mission San Miguel Arcángel
801 Mission Street
San Miguel, CA 93451-0069
805-467-3256

(p. 28) Mission San Antonio de Padua
Hunter Liggett Military Reservation
Jolon, CA 93928
831-385-4478

(p. 30) Nuestra Señora de La Soledad
36641 Fort Romie Road
Soledad, CA 93960
831-678-2586   closed Tuesdays

(p. 31) Mission San Carlos Borromeo del Río Carmelo
3080 Rio Road
Carmel, CA 93923
831-624-3600

(p. 33) Mission San Juan Bautista
2nd and Mariposa Streets
San Juan Bautista, CA 95045
831-623-4528

(p. 35) Mission Santa Cruz
126 High Street
Santa Cruz, CA 95060
831-426-5686

(p. 37) Mission Santa Clara de Asís
Santa Clara University
500 El Camino Real, Box 3217
Santa Clara, CA 95053-3217
408-554-4023

(p. 39) Mission San José
43300 Mission Blvd
Fremont, CA 94539
510-657-1797

(p. 40) Mission San Francisco de Asís (Mission Dolores)
3321 16th Street
San Francisco, CA 94114
415-621-8203

(p. 41) The Sanchez Adobe
1000 Linda Mar Blvd
Pacifica, CA 94044
650-359-1462

(p. 42) Mission San Rafael Arcánge
1104 Fifth Avenue
San Rafael, CA 94901
415-454-8141

(p. 44) San Francisco Solano SHP (Sonoma Mission)
114 East Spain Street
Sonoma, CA 95476
707-938-9560